Heather Henning and Alison Atkins

When God Created the World

Lots of little flaps for little fingers!

In the beginning darkness was everywhere.

God said, "Let there be light!"
And so light shone into the darkness.

Now there was day and night.

God created the air and the sky—

an enormous sky, with fluffy clouds.

He made the wide oceans and the deep seas.

He made rolling waves and splashing spray.

5

God made dry land—
the high hills and the tall mountains,

6

the deep valleys and the wide plains.
God saw it, and he was pleased
with the land he had created.

"Now let grasses, trees, and plants of every kind
grow on the earth," said God.

There were tall trees, small trees, bushes, and fruit trees;
8   redwood, maple, cherry, and oak; apple, banana, pear, and pine.

There were climbing plants
and prickly plants,
and waving grasses,
ripe with corn.

There were flowers everywhere.
Red, yellow, orange, purple, pink, and blue,
they scented the air.

Lilies, lavender, daisies, roses, and honeysuckle.
God was pleased with all the growing things he had created.

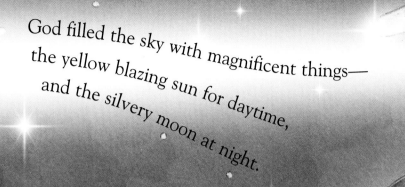

God filled the sky with magnificent things—
the yellow blazing sun for daytime,
and the silvery moon at night.

He gave the comets fiery tails.

He made millions of twinkling stars
to shine in the darkness of space.
And God was pleased with what he had created.

13

"Let there be living things in the water," said God.
So he made schools of fish
to swim in his vast oceans:

big fish, little fish, round fish, flat fish—
so many flapping tails and waving fins!

14

He made teeny-tiny sea-creatures
and great big sea-monsters.
And God was pleased
with the swimming things
he had created.

15

"Let there be living things in the air," said God.
So he filled the air
with millions of birds and insects.

16

They had wings
that go whirr, buzz, and hum.
Birds with feathers
bright as the morning sun,

and butterflies and busy bees
flew through the heavens.
And God was pleased
with the flying things he had created.

"Let there be living things on the earth,"
said God.
So God created lots of animals—all different.

Animals that were furry, smooth, stripy, spotted,
wild, or friendly, God made them all.
Soon they were running, jumping, galloping and hopping,

slithering, bouncing, climbing and leaping
all over God's world.
And God was pleased with the animals he had created.

Last of all, God created people.
"Let there be people!" said God.
And God made the first man and called him Adam;
and he made the first woman and called her Eve.

He made them to be his friends,
and he asked them to take care of this world.
God was very, very pleased with everything he had created.

God loved the world he had created,
and he loved everything in it.
And after that, God rested.

Copyright © 2003 Anno Domini Publishing

1 Churchgates, The Wilderness, Berkhamsted, Herts HP4 2UB
Text copyright © 2003 Heather Henning
Illustrations copyright © 2003 Alison Atkins
Editorial Director Annette Reynolds
Art Director Gerald Rogers
Production John Laister
ISBN: 978-1-59325-077-5

First published in the US and Canada by The Word Among Us Press in 2006
9639 Doctor Perry Road Ijamsville, Maryland 21754
www.wordamongus.org
800-775-9673

11 10 09 08 07   2 3 4 5 6

Printed and bound in China